Gallery Of One

Gallery Of One

HOWARD BELL

MainSpring Books

Printed in the United States of America

ISBN 979-8-89114-160-5 (sc)
ISBN 979-8-89114-162-9 (e)

Library of Congress Pre-assigned Control Number: 2024926919

2025.02.25

MainSpring Books
5901 W. Century Blvd
Suite 750
Los Angeles, CA, US, 90045

www.mainspringbooks.com

Gallery Of Memories

As I roam through my gallery of memories each day,
That collection of misery so wretched and poor,
all those sad, empty dreams, framed in unfaithful schemes,
Line the walls of each corridor.
I'd never roam through this gallery of misery, my dear,
Were it not, for one priceless work of art.
It's a portrait of you and the warm, tender love
That flowed from your unselfish heart.
I'll continue to roam through this gallery, my dear,
Until this heart's lonely cries are heard there no more.
I'll roam night and day through each passageway,
As my tears, slowly cover the floor.
Were it not for that one priceless portrait of you
And the warm love that lived here before,
I'd close this gallery of sad, empty dreams
and forever seal up the door.

Seasons Of Love

You brought love to my life the first time we met, the sight of you filled my young heart with spring. The touch of your hand seemed to make the flowers grow, your voice caused the songbirds to sing. Our love grew as warm as the mid-summer sun, your kisses gave summer it's start. In the warmth of our love, not once did I dream that father time would pull us apart.

Like autumn, your love began slowly to change. I felt lonely, though I didn't know why.

Like the breezes of fall, you grew cooler each day.

I watched as our love slowly withered and died.

As your love became colder, I knew winter had come.

Your restless heart would soon have to go.

When you left, you took, the spring from my life and left my heart as cold as the snow.

Winds of Love

I remember why I learned to fly, upon the winds of love. I recall the fall from down below to regions up above. I've left the ground, and I can't come down, even if I wanted to. Why should I try when I can fly on winds of love with you? Wise men know how things below fall down from up above. But I know why I'm falling up since you taught me to love. I can fly so high, I can touch the sky, and soar the heavens blue, on winds of love you gave to me, when I fell in love with you. On winds of love, I'm up above the world and all its woes. The fears and cares of yesteryears now seem so far below. I've left the ground, and I can't come down, even if I wanted to.
Why should I try when I can fly on winds of love with you.

The Habit

Your longing eyes and trembling lips make my heart
leap wild within, makes me want to take all caution and
cast it to the wind. But a dream like you would break my
heart into the moment I awake. And to lose your love
after loving you would be more than I could take. A kiss
would lead to greater need that I could not control. And
my heart would start to yearn, dear, to the bottom of my soul.
This forbidden fruit, here within my reach, is something I must
never take.

For I know you would become a habit, a habit, I could never
break.

A Night like This

Do you remember, my darling, this night long ago, when we fell in love in the moon's silvery glow? You held me so tightly, our hearts beat so fast, tonight we'll relive, that love from the past. Thanks to you, my eyes opened, and love found our hearts. That love's still ours, and will never depart. Now we're blessed, with a night, so like one before. And tonight you and I, share those moments, once more.

Ton of Love

To me, you'll always be a ten and also number one. If love was measured by the pound, your share, would weigh a ton.

Are You Making Believe

When I'm with you my darling, I can't help myself,
I must trust you to show me the way.
One look in your eyes, and I become hypnotized,
when you touch me, I couldn't tell the night from
the day.
When you hold me, my darling, I lose all track
of time.
When you kiss me, I hear wedding bells chime.
I beg you, my darling, don't let me be deceived.
Don't make me believe you love me,
If you're only making believe.

Autumn and Fall

O autumn, so lovingly bathed in the dew,
how great are the honors bestowed upon you.

The fulfillment of seasons and harvest entwine,
from your bountiful table, God's creatures shall dine.

O autumn, so colorful, so majestically grand, you received
special blessings from God's loving hand.

You've been honored with twin names, autumn and fall,
could it be you're the loveliest season of all.

Autumn Love

You remind me of an autumn day, with leaves falling down,
Hair like golden fields of wheat, eyes of chestnut brown.

Lips as red as maple leaves, moist as autumn dew,
I've always loved an autumn day, maybe that's why I love you.

Your kiss is like the autumn sun that drinks the morning dew,
your touch is like a fireside, it warms me through and through.

Your love takes me to places and times I loved so dear, each
day becomes an autumn day the moment you appear.

Bat and Batty

I went to a movie show just to have some place to go.
It was about this real cool cat who could change into a bat.
He used a coffin for a bed to make think that he was dead,
but as soon as the moon would rise, he would open up his
eyes. He wore a long black velvet cape that could take on
any shape, he could draw it across his face and vanish
without a trace. When he changed into a man, he wore a
ring on his right hand. The magic in that ring could make a
chick do anything.
That sucker had wicked eyes, those eyes could hypnotize.
He had a paralyzing smile that drove those maidens wild.
His upper cuspids had such charm, chicks would fall right in his arms.
He would bite that jugular vein and drive those gals insane.
Once that sucker made his score, they kept coming back for more.
The only way to kill that clown was to stake him to the ground.
They took a great big wooden dart and drove it through that
sucker's heart. I ain't never seen a bat like that.

Cactus Country Cowboy

Cactus country cowboy, ride until
the sun runs out of time.
Desert tanned and calloused hands,
earning every dollar to the dime.
Cactus country cowboy, the moon will soon
rise in the western sky.
The breeze will turn the tumble weed,
the stars will put a twinkle in your eyes.
Your guitar strings will bring that
lonesome coyote to the stage to sing along.
Your pony is nodding peaceful now,
patiently waiting for your song.
Cactus country cowboy, ride until
the sun runs out of time.
Cactus country cowboy, earning every dollar
to the dime.

Computerized Love

This match wasn't made up in heaven,
but it was made somewhere up above.
Some place way up in cyber space
with high-speed computerized love.
Sweet heart, you're tripping my breakers,
more love than I'm able to use,
your sweet love is pulling at lease sixty
amps, mine has a thirty-amp fuse.
You're killing my kilowatt meter,
It's spinning around and around,
if we ever short circuit in that water bed,
we'll trip every breaker in town.
High-speed computerized love
Sure gave my libido a shove,
Over loading my circuits every time
that we kiss, and I don't have the
ohms to resist.

Counterfeit Love

You can't turn love off like a candle
Each time a little wind blows.
The flower of love's ever growing,
it blooms sunshine or snow. True
love rolls with the punches
Through hell or heaven above.
If you love only in good times,
What you have is counterfeit love.
Counterfeit love can't take it,
the heartaches a cruel world can bring.
It flickers and dies in the teardrops and
ceases to burn in the rain.
If you've been saving your whole life through
for that star studded mansion in the heavens
of blue,
be sure that your savings are good up above. You
can't shop in heaven with counterfeit love.

Down Home Party

Come on, and bring your chicky baby,
Bring along your dancing shoes.
We're having, a down-home party,
we're going to dance away all those
blues.
All night long, from dusk till dawn,
we're doing the down-home boogie.
We'll do, the spunky chicken too,
we'll do, the cluck cluck, and the
clucklebuck,
And the cockle doodle doodle do.
All night long, from dusk till dawn,
Betsy, she's the chicky baby.
Barney, he's the cock of the walk.
When Betsy says cluck, Barney does the cluckel
buck.
Then we boogie till the feathers fall, all night long,
from dusk till dawn.

Field Of Sin

Don't plow in another man's field, son.
Don't sow in another man's soil.
For the seed sown in sin must be reaped in the end,
with unyielding, heart-breaking toil.
There's no escape from the harvest of sin, son.
It must be reaped to the grave and beyond.
The chains of deceit lay sore on the feet, and
none can escape from the pain they have sown.
Plow only the field that God gives you.
Sow your seed in the soil of the just.
Let truth, rule your heart,
That sin may depart.
Your neighbors' fence will be built out of trust.
The harvest you reap will be bountiful,
with the fruits that sweeten life's race.
You'll walk in the light,
Stumble not in the night, with no bitter harvest to face.

In the Past

My present has no future since our love is in the past,
you were my one and only love dear, my first and my last.
As you drift toward your future, the past is where I'll be.
There, our love remains forever, sealed inside a memory.

As you live all your tomorrows, I'll relive our
yesterdays.
Without your love, I have no future, so the past is where
I'll stay.
If you find you ever need me, you know where I will be.
In the past when you still loved me, holding fast your
memory.
If your future brings you sorrow, please return to yesterday.

If you need me, just remember, your heart will point the way.
I won't be hard to find dear you know where I will be.
I'll remain here where you left me, holding fast your memory.

Living on leftover love

I've been living on left over love,
I can't wait to take off these gloves,
I've used up the memories, but we'll
make some new when I get these
two hands full of you.
Baby keep that fire burning, your
wandering man is returning.
I'll need some new memories
to give me a shove, while I'm living
on leftover love.
Baby, I'm hungry as hell, I miss your
good cooking as well, but I'm in the mood
for more than good food.
I've been living on leftover love.
Put on that black negligee, pat down that
sexy sachet.
I'm one twenty-nine from that sweet
homey line, and living on leftover love.

Life's old recipe

There's an old recipe that helps us to see
Our future in a clear, simple way.
Add one cup of sorrow to every tomorrow
for each evil deed done today.
To each day of sadness, add one cup of gladness
for an act of love along the way.
Charity is the seasoning of life, that sweetens life's
bitter race,
but the hateful and greedy, who prey on the needy,
have bitter tomorrows to face.
If your days have turned bitter, stop and consider
the seasoning you use on the way.
We spice each tomorrow, with gladness or sorrow,
we're preparing, our future each day.
We don't need fortune tellers,
it's easy to see just follow life's old recipe.

Maybe Love Is

Since Adam and Eve, men have wondered, what is this strange thing called love.

In love, we fall toward heaven,

And heaven is always above.

Wise men know how things fall below, all things fall down from above, except one thing that keeps falling up. What is this strange thing called love?

MAYBE LOVE IS, the answer to questions that trouble the heart.

MAYBE LOVE IS, the transport on which heaven's chosen depart.

MAYBE LOVE IS, the pathway to heaven's secret abode.

MAYBE LOVE IS, the helper sent to lighten our load.

No one really knows what love is, the wisest of men could not say.

We only know when souls go to heaven, love's always leading the way.

MAYBE LOVE IS, beyond human thought, as a heavenly work of art.

MAYBE LOVE IS, so simple, it can only be known by the heart.

MAYBE LOVE IS, the fountain of youth to all who thirst for life.

MAYBE LOVE IS, the river of truth that cover the stones of strife.

MAYBE LOVE IS, all of these things to all loving souls who believe.

MAYBE LOVE, has much more to give than some have the faith to receive.

MAYBE LOVE IS, the gateway to heaven, or maybe the key to the door.

WHATEVER LOVE IS, there seems little doubt it's always worth falling for.

Medley One

Sea of Love

My tears fall in silence, not a sound, when I weep.
The sea of love, has no measure, still water run's deep.

Life's evil Seed

All are born into a world of sin, for some, there's death's early sleep,
having not yet sown, of life's evil seed, with no bitter harvest, to reap,

Charity

Charity, begins at home, my friend, I've heard it said, time and again.
But why does charity seem always to end, at the very same place
where it's said to begin.

Love's Sale

Everything is half off, and that includes me. All heartaches on clearance,
buy one, get one free. Everything has to go, all my dreams, hopes and
cares, I still have some memories, but I'm all out of tears. I'll consider all
offers by phone or by mail. Better yet, stop by, my going out of love sale.

Medley Two

Cowboy Moon

His heart is running north with her, his tears are running south.
He's running from a life of crime, and time is running out. That
blood-red sun will soon be heading west toward high noon,
goodbye, goodbye, cowboy moon.

Key of death

Death, O death, are you the key that unlock the prisons and set
spirits free? These prisons of flesh, with bars made of bone, we
serve time together, yet always alone.

Sad Song

It doesn't matter if I splatter, when I fall down from this ladder, or if I
get hung on a rung. Just remember, when it's over, and I fertilize the
clover, you'll forget about this sad song that I sung.

Dreams Tell lies

I dreamed I lost you to someone new, I searched a dim-lit world for you.
Afraid and lonely, oh how I cried, tell me love is true and dreams tell lies.

To my Valentine

When love is shared with one so fair,
so sweet, so kind as you,
love need not roam
love loves at home,
today, and ever true.

Medley Three

Fool over You

It's always the same, each time I complain and accuse you of breaking the rules. The way you sigh, with those tears in your eyes, you're so good at making me feel like a fool. What is it with you I don't understand, why be so kind all the time? Did you not learn any rudeness in school? You're so good at making me feel like a fool.

Youth

Youth is the springtime of life, the time for sowing the seed of our fate. But time for harvest tarries not long, the time for bitter reaping won't wait.

Neighbor

Has my world so narrowed, I'd forgotten to heed one of the greatest commandments our heavenly Father decreed. Have I loved only those, my neighbors in name, and forgotten my neighbor indeed. Little wonder I'd forgotten, seems I saw him just once in my hour of very great need.

Wandering Neighbors

Souls of the road are neighbors indeed, like the Samaritan of old, an unforgettable breed.

Epitaph

This lonesome writer departed too soon. This man stirred hell with a paper spoon.

Medley Four

Love in the tears

A flower must have a little sunshine, a heart needs a shelter from fear.
They wither and die unattended, like love left to long in the tears.
Love left to long in the teardrops will flicker and die like a flame.
The ashes are carried away with the wind and buried like dust in the rain.
A child needs love, shelter, and food. A friend needs a hand now and then.
A woman needs the touch of her man to keep the flame burning within.

God's Love

There are no heights, no widths, no depths God's love does not transcend.
So great is God's unselfish love, no man can comprehend. To invoke the
mighty love of God is the highest wisdom of man. Before his all -consuming
wrath, what mortal man can stand.

The Will

I made my will out this morning, I'm leaving it all to you. After careful
consideration, I felt that's what I must do. I feel you deserve it all, dear
everything that I have to you. Since I couldn't afford a postage stamp,
I'm sending it postage due.

Miracles Denied

We make God's greatest gift to man of little or no worth,
when an unborn child is denied by man the miracle of
birth.
Who has the right to say to these, you have no right to
live.
Who has the right to take away that which they did not
give.
Men have stood for every cause since God gave life to man,
and gave him power to procreate and fill this barren land.
For causes just and unjust, many nations war hath torn.
Should not a man now take a stand for the helpless yet
unborn.
Where are the brave, the strong in heart, when the helpless
need a friend? Who will plead the cause for these, unable yet
to fend?
Will we not take their cause to heart, while our hearts beat
within.
Can we allow their hearts be stilled and still be known as men.

#

Nothing at the end of the rainbow but rain.
Nothing at the end of the railroad but train.
Nothing at the end of the highway but signs, and
I ain't lost nothing, cause nothings still mine.

Nothing at the end of a dream but a sigh.
Nothing upon the horizon but sky.
Nothing in the past or the future but time, and I
ain't lost nothing, cause nothings still mine.

North of the border, south of a quarter,
a nickel and dimer, a likely life timer.
North of the border, south of a quarter, and
nothing but nothing between.

One more kiss

One more kiss before I go away,
then let me hear you say,
we'll kiss again someday. And
every night, I'll say a prayer for you,
pray God will see us through, until
I come home to you.
The time draws near, but let there be no tears,
though weeks turn into years,
our love will not grow cold.
For space and time are just a state of mind.
Our hearts remain entwined,
true love forever binds.
The seven seas could not keep us apart
someday, I'll find a way
to come to you, sweetheart.
Always believe, although we say goodbye,
our love will see us through.
True love can never die.

Out of Love Sale

Everything is half off, and that includes me.
Heartaches on clearance, buy one, get one free.
Everything has to go, all my dreams, hopes, and
cares. I still have some memories, but I'm all out of
tears. I'll consider all offers, by phone or by mail,
better yet, stop by my going out of love sale.

Raindrops and teardrops

Listen to the raindrops they're playing our song,
aren't they so like the many teardrops we've cried.
How many have fallen through the dark, stormy years,
as our love slowly withered and died.
The clouds of distrust over shadowed our hearts,
leaving only cold darkness within.
The cruel winds of pride blew our conscience aside,
our wounded love having no chance to win,
it's been so long since we've loved,
I just can't remember when or where our love first went wrong.
But those cold, chilling raindrops
somehow bring it to mind,
It's as though, they are playing
our song.
Listen to the raindrops,
they're playing our song.

Reading Between The Teardrops

Broken hearts can't always find phrases
for feelings they need to convey.
But if you could read between the teardrops,
you could read what my heart needs to say.

Words don't always come easy for feelings we
need to impart, but it's all written here,
between the teardrops, in lines running
straight from the heart.

Seed of Love

Have you sown your precious seed, the seed of love. It's the gift we share
from heaven up above. If you wish to reap your share, of this gift so
fine and rare,
you must carefully sow your seed within the heart, and water oh so gently
from the start.
Watch it grow a flower, so lovely and
so fair,
all the beauty on Gods earth will not compare.
Treat this precious seed as manna from above,
it's the precious gift of life we know and love. It
will in time become the tree of life,
when sown between a husband and
his wife.

Sleepy Eyes

I found your note the night you went away,
it's strange how much a few short words
can say.
One thing's for sure, they made me realize
how much I couldn't see through sleepy eyes.
Sleepy eyes don't sleep much anymore,
they read your note and watch me walk the floor.
Sometimes, they see a star fall from the sky, and
wish they'd only dreamed you said goodbye.
Instead of dreams, my nights bring memories,
the sand man, hardly ever visits me.
It's hard to sleep when memories make you cry,
those tears sure have a way with sleepy eyes.
Sleepy eyes don't sleep much anymore, they
read your note and watch me walk the floor.
Sometimes they see a star fall from the sky, and
wish they'd only dreamed you said good bye.

Songs of the Lonely

Listen to the songs of the lonely, listen to the sad tales they tell.
Learn from songs of the left all alone, don't make the mistakes
of loves that have failed.
Listen to the songs of the lonely, let them teach us how love goes
astray.
Learn from the songs of the left all alone, let them help us keep love from
harm's way.
Let them teach us how kind hearts are broken, let them teach us
how love is lost.
They bought their education at a very high price. If we listen,
they will save us the cost.
They all seem to say, don't travel this way,
don't travel this highway of pain.
Don't make the mistakes that I've made,
they all share this lonely refrain.

Springtime

Oh, beautiful springtime, so sweet and so fair,
with your fragrance of blossoms filling the air.
Our creator hath blessed you, with beauty untold,
in you, allows so much life to unfold.

All creatures are busily gathering their food,
the birds too, are lovingly hatching their brood.

The seedlings unfold from the life-giving womb.
Of the seed born last autumn, beneath the
bright harvest moon.

O springtime so lovely, too soon you are gone,
but you gave birth to summer, we're not left alone.

Fair thee well lovely springtime, so precious, so dear.
Should our creator be willing, I shall greet thee next year.

Summer

Oh, beautiful summer, the mother of fall, so dearly
beloved by the great and the small.
With your warm, loving nature, there's small wonder why
God bestowed such great beauty in the mid-summer sky.
Entrusting to you each tender young thing,
so gently brought forth in the mist of the spring.
Like a kind, loving mother, you nurtured them all,
delivering them safely to harvest in fall.
We'll miss you oh summer, dear kind, loving friend.
How greatly God blessed us when you he did send.

Winter

The beauty of winter is not often told, many see winter as bitter and cold.
But I fancy winter, the best time of year, with numerous pleasures I treasure
so dear.
It's a time of reflection and strengthening of heart, as you plan for the spring
when a new life will start.
You feel so alive in your warm winter clothes, as the fresh, chilling breeze
gently
sting at your nose.

The excitement you feel, so deeply within, as your home is buffeted by
the cold winter wind.

You watch out your window as snow's falling down, transforming
surroundings as it covers the ground.

There's nothing so lovely as moonlight's soft glow, on the velvet smooth
surface of a fresh winter's snow. There's beauty in summer, spring time,
and fall, but the beauty of winter surpasses them all.

You filled up my life

My life lacked direction, I was drifting along, didn't care where I was going, didn't care where I'd gone. Thanks to you, that's behind me, I found a new life when you told me you loved me, and you'd be my wife. My life once was empty, now it's full as can be. You filled up my life, when you walked out on me. With a heart full of pain, two eyes filled with tears, enough sorrow to last me for two hundred years. My wild days are over, all in the past, you gave me direction and a future at last.
You filled up my life when you walked out on me, I wish I could give you what you gave to me.

Wild ROSE

The songs of the lonely
are filled with the tales
of hearts that were broken
into. Some hearts were
reckless, some too young to
know, that rivers of teardrops
won't tame a wild rose.
It lives for the moonlight,
it drinks from the dew.
It opens its heart to the
breeze. .Its love then is carried
where err the wind blows,
and rivers of teardrops, won't tame a wild rose.
Wild, wild rose, so lovely and free,
how I'd love to keep you with me.
But hearts break too easy and
pain leaves so slow,
and rivers of teardrops
won't tame a wild rose.
Goodbye, GOD keep you, wild rose.

Wife

I felt I should tell you, my sweet darling wife, how I've cherished
your presence through most of my life.

Like the fragrance of springtime, you've scented my days, your love warms my
heart as the suns summer rays. The beauty of autumn can hardly compare to
the beauty I see in your soft flowing hair. You're so lovely to look at, so tender,
so fair, yet your courage and strength with the mighty compare.

When life's paths were treacherous and difficult to tread, your bravery
sustained me and urged me ahead. Through you, God hath blessed me my
sweet darling wife, through you I've been granted continuing life. So freely
you've given, asking naught in return, the flame of your love ceased never
to burn. I could never repay you, not even in part, but know dear, I love
you with all of my heart.

Who are my Kin

Is this not my brother, the son of my father, and my sister from my mother's womb.

Should I concern myself, with the rest of mankind, in my heart would there be room. If my conscience is clear toward these, my kin, with the rest of mankind, need I bother.

Oh yes, I perceive all those humble souls who do the will of our Heavenly father.

Whisper of Love

Wrap your love in a whisper, sealed with your lips,
safe from all who stand in our way,
hold me closer than flowers hold the new fallen dew,
until dawn turns the night into day.
Whisper, whisper, of love, locked in two hearts
yours and mine,
wrap your love in a whisper, safe from the listener,
sealed in the secret of time.
Wrap your love in a whisper, soft as your lips,
with your heart, send it quietly to me.
Hold me closer than flowers hold the
new fallen dew, until dawn causes moon beams to
flee.

Were You Pretending

Were you pretending when you left me dear,
the way you smiled and walked away,
you seemed so happy when you left, my dear,
and I loved seeing you that way.
Were you pretending when you told me dear,
that you now love somebody new,
please tell me that you were pretending,
don't leave me so alone and blue.
I won't mind if you're just making believe
my dear,
I love to see you having fun,
remember how you used to tease me dear,
and say to me, you're not the one.
Please tell me that you're just pretending now,
and this is just some silly game,
because if you're not just pretending, my tears will
drop like falling rain.

Vessel Of Love

Darling, I brought you here for a reason tonight,
I felt the seashore was the place we should be.
There are some things I must ask you, though
it's breaking my heart,
you know I love you, so be truthful with me,
take my hand, hold it tightly, and don't look away,
if you love me, we can weather the storm,
but our loves being threatened by deception and lies, as
a ship when the tempest has formed.
Our love is our vessel on life's stormy sea,
our refuge from the depths of despair,
it was formed out of truth, the essence of love,
and sealed with the trust we both share.
Lies are the icebergs on life's stormy sea, and
falsehoods cause the tempest to blow. If our loves
being threatened by deception and lies,
my darling, you must let me know.
Take my hand, hold it tightly, and don't look away,
if you love me, we can weather the storm. But time's
growing short dear, repairs must be made before the
new tempest has formed.

Thank You Lord

I confess Lord, I've been something less than grateful,
I've even thought at times that you had let me down.
If you'll forgive me, I'll try to do things better,
and just be patient until my turn comes around.
You see, her loss was more than I could take Lord,
the thought of losing her was hard for me to bare.
In my grief, I nearly lost the faith Lord,
I even thought at times, what good comes out of prayer.
Forgive me Lord, for doubting in your kindness,
forever thinking you had turned your back on me.
I'll remain here till my turn comes up in heaven,
until you are ready I'll remain here patiently.
In my dream, I saw her by the living fountain,
in the flowering garden near the tree of life,
I saw her strolling down the golden streets of heaven,
then I recalled this lovely creature, was my wife.
I saw her smile the way she smiled when I first met her,
and pain no longer marked her lovely brow.
Thank you Jesus, for that brief glimpse into heaven,
though I'm lonely, I feel so much better now.

Take Me To Love

Speak to me softly, tell me you care, promise your love
will always be there.
Hold me and kiss me softly and then, take me to places
where I've never been.
Show me where loves flame first knew its glow,
show me the garden where loves flower grows,
where petals of love lay soft as the dew, and
feather a love nest made only for two.
Let your arms surround me like moonbeams in fall,
yet strong as the gemstones that form heavens wall.
Hold me and kiss me softly and then, take me to places
where I've never been.
Patiently guide me through loves secret door,
to places where true love resides ever more.
Show me where loves flame first knew its glow,
show me the garden where loves flower grows.
Let love settle on me soft as the dew,
take me to love dear, take me with you.